AF571874

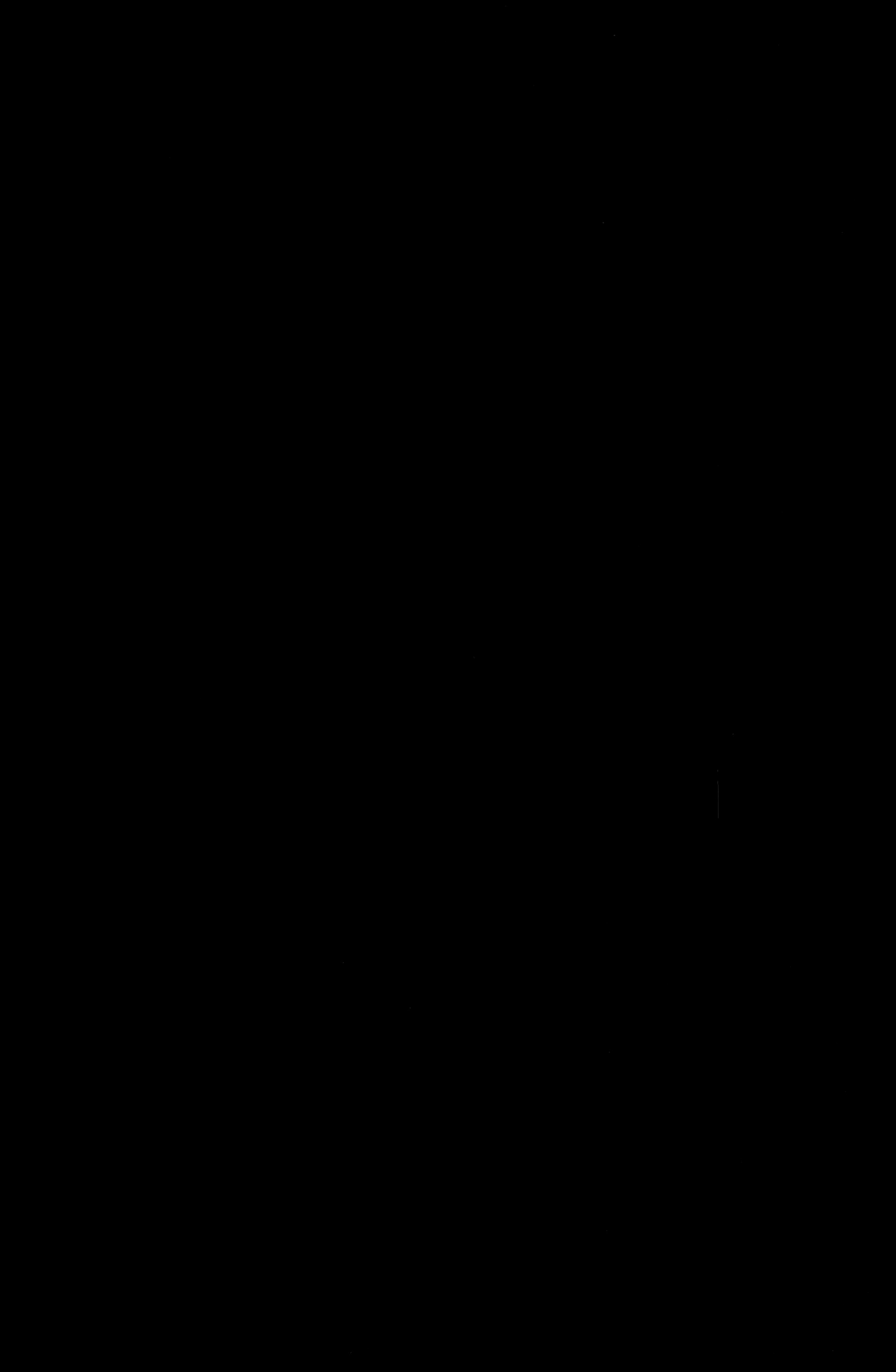

SIRENS' SONGS
ELISABETH STEVENS

SIRENS' SONGS

LIVRE D'ARTISTE FACSIMILE

ELISABETH STEVENS

SIRENS' SONGS

Editor: Clarinda Harriss
Graphic design: Ace Kieffer
Front cover art: Elisabeth Stevens
Back cover photograph: Laura Schleussner

Cover and illustrations are original copper plate etchings by the Author.

BrickHouse Books, Inc. 2011
306 Suffolk Road
Baltimore, MD 21218

Distributor: Itasca Books, Inc.
© 2011

ISBN: 978-1-935916-03-1

Printed in the United States of America

Acknowledgements: Some of these poems have appeared in *Centennial Review, Confrontation, Late Knocking, Maryland Poetry Review, New Voices, Scribble, The Lyric.*

"The heart is deceitful above all things and beyond cure. Who can understand it?"

Jeremiah 17:9

"Your path led through the sea, your way through mighty waters, though your footprints were not seen."

Psalm 77:19

TABLE OF CONTENTS

Poems

ONE

TWO

THREE

FOUR

Etchings

ONE

White

WHITE

Bright, bright
white in the tide pools,
white breaking over the ledges,

lifting rock strands of seaweed,
drawing back in foam lines, spreading,
rising to break with green.

High white
with celadon streaks,
break high bright white white.

SIREN'S SONG

The rocks below are sharp,
the tides are breaking high,
I call to you to come to me,
put out your frail white boat to sea
and come, and come
and sail your boat to die.

The fog is white as death,
it rises from the sea,
my hair curls long, my skin shines soft,
I sing to you to come to me,
to ride to me, to haste to me
to die.

I see your bow rise up
and break between black waves.
You swim to me, you float to me,
you lie with me–as others have–
so pale, so clean, so cold,
they die...they die...they die....

MAINE SUMMER

The branches of the old elms
hang down loose
and swing so green and sing.

The sound is loose–like waterfalls,
the sky is loose–the clouds spread wide
in milkweed wisps and twirls of foam.

Summer is loose–yards of chiffon–
white folds trail out so long and light
and float to sea at fall.

MAINE STREAM

Up beyond the barn
in the meadow bordered by tall pines
a stream flows towards the sea.

Down at the inlet,
when it's low tide, you can see
the muddy, twisting course.

They say the sweetest clams
grow in that bed of fresh water
under the tides.

Floating Hair

FLOATING HAIR

On the sea porch,
ten o'clock July,
I am combing–
warm hands combing–
my long hair loose to sun.

Some copper curling hairs,
alone, or snarled and knotted,
sail lightly over the low railing
to catch on green thorns
of beach roses among bees.

Others float further,
twine in tallest grasses,
flutter from white tufts,
or rest on dark rock teeth
at the inlet by the tide line.

Sun, sun,
my red rays are everywhere.
They too are inexhaustible–
rising, curling,
shining, growing.

WILD LUPINES

Lie down in brown leaf tangles
in the overgrown seaside garden.
Look up at the sky through lupines,
purple spires against the sun disk,
sea blue spires touched with white,
a few pink spires, a few pure white.

Six foot yellow sap-channel stalks,
armed with red at the bottom,
have short, sparse, silver bristles
near the moist green root mounds
where fragile white spiders and
energetic black ants thrive.

Lupine leaves–fierce, pointed ovals,
palmate with thin center veins–
spread below as many as twenty
florets with pollen-bloated bee cups
that cradle pale, notched pods. There
soft green seeds sleep side by side.

Warm, waiting to blossom, waiting
to rise, the lupines thrust upward as
flesh sinks farther into damp, dark soil,
almost willing–yes, willing–to let lupines,
strong purple, blue, pink and white lupines,
wild lupines, eclipse midsummer sun.

LEAVING ALL MEANINGS

Leaving all meanings behind,
to go quietly, drained of fear,
to an empty field above a quiet sea
and there, to rest side by side
without words and without questions:
this, in one day of a lifetime,
is sufficient.

ON THE SEA PORCH

The fog is burning off at ten o'clock
and streaming out to sea.
Sounds multiply.
It is impossible to distinguish
the hammer from the echo.
Distant dog barks are faint–
but clear as farthest elms.

Wet white webs adorn
the tallest grasses, and
a creature impossible to see
scurries in the roots' tangle.
A fly buzzes, circles my head.
Someone across the road
laughs twice.

Bees work in jewel weed,
strip sweetness from purple nightshade.
A black butterfly lingers
on an orange flower.
I hear you breathing,
inside, still asleep.

Mermaid

THE MERMAID'S TALE

I was born from the sea. The first difficulty was seaweed. Seaweed slides above easily in long, glistening tendrils when you are under the waves. When I had to rise, seaweed held me in yellow-brown, restraining arms, weighting my shoulders.

Somehow, I reached the surface. When I knew what air was, I realized that if I were dragged back I would drown. I was dragged back. Seaweed tightened like a noose. Long shadows I had known and loved in the depths pulled at my body.

The water–how sweet and frightening it seemed. It was deliciously warm near the surface, much warmer than where I had been, but to stay was to drown. I struggled, breathed, was drawn back. Repeatedly, I fought for air–only to go under for what might have been the last time.

Finally, I breathed easily. I was lying on the beach exhausted, washed by the receding tide. After I had rested, I began to sing.

SHORTCUT

The way to the blueberries
everybody knows
is the old tar road
that winds around the inlet.

I know a shortcut.
Climb the steep sand cliff
above the stone point beach.
You'll discover

the trail no one remembers
rising through beach roses
between black spike branches
of dead pines. Soon

you're right in the middle of
the juiciest patch of ripe ones.
From up there, you can see
dolphins playing beyond the breakers.

Later, when you're hot and stained and
sunburned and your pails are full to
brimming, raise a purple palm and
signal to me swimming in deep water.

Then, riding on a wave crest,
I'll cut short my sea time, Blue Boy.
By the shortcut, I'll rise to you,
wet and eager, hungry to raid your spoils.

WEBS

Webs mask morning grass.
Fog flattens the hills, hides
dry elms. Sounds carry.

Across the inlet, someone
is crying. Harsh words
cross the water. Salt fog

spreads like anger, leaves
flesh chilled and pimply.
Voices beseech their own echoes,

hands grope, grasp air.
Damp feet slide, then falter,
memory fades and blurs.

Enmeshed in webs we do not see,
we are silenced by voices
we will not hear.

SEA STONES

These cloud grey stones
scattered at the water's edge
turn midnight black
when tide rises.

Sea-smoothed,
heavy and cornerless,
this moon-shaped weight
just fits my palm.

Carried from
incoherent arrangement,
it will be a lodestone singer:
"Come back, come home to the sea."

SUMMER FLIES

This old grey house
has one white-rimmed window
facing the sea.

On the paint-peeled sill,
left from last summer,
flies.

Legs curled,
they lie on their backs,
rearranged by winds.

Lost days
wash back
like warm tides.

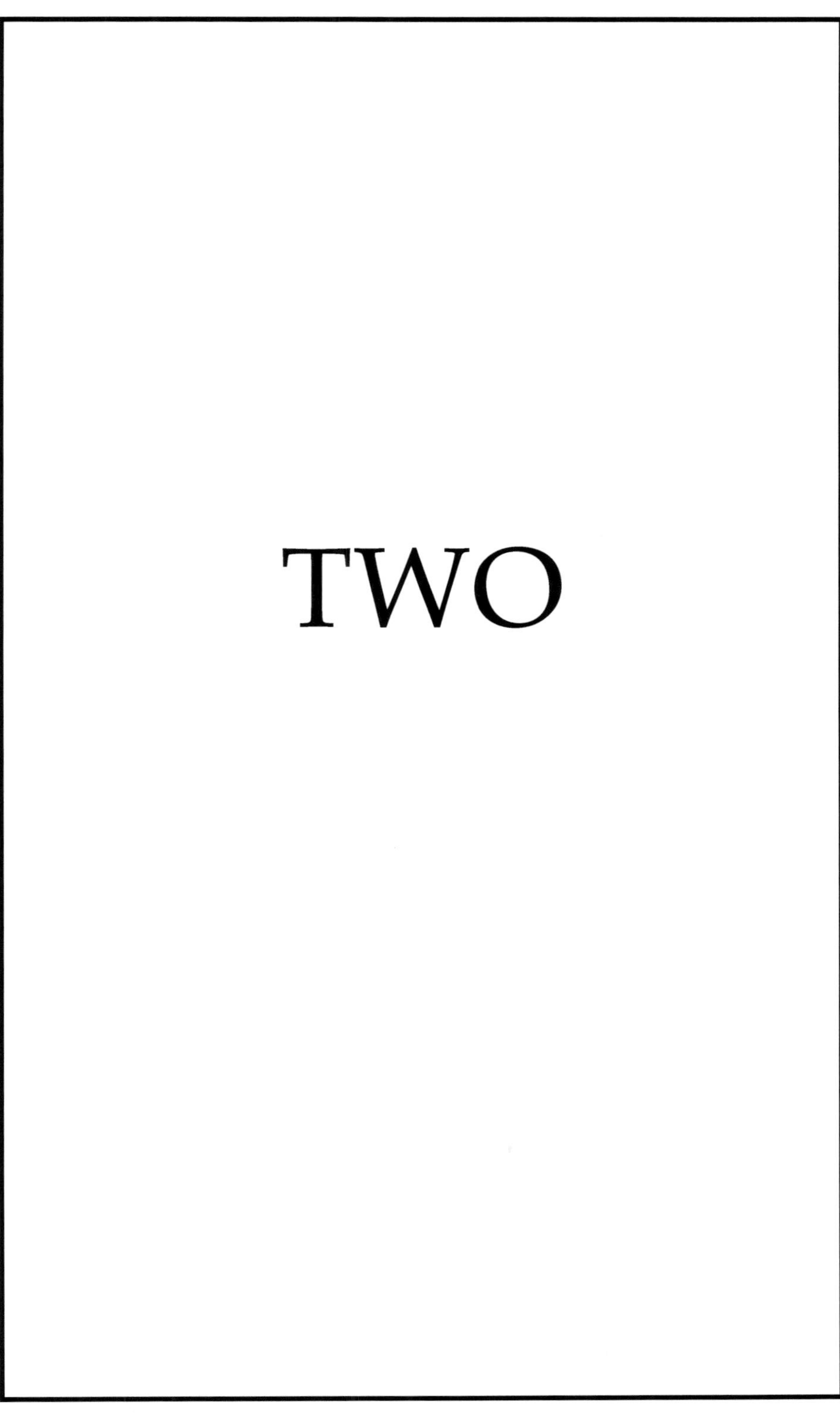

TWO

LINES FROM A PLAY
(The Virgin Speaks)

I will not tell you who I am.
I do not like these tedious wintry plays–
cold masks their silly couplets babbling on.
Give me my comb, a mirror here, and I'll
devise a face–not for these sad-shanked poets,
whose weak rhymes tickle when they should be
strong,
and jingle on when they should die, and go,
not paying what is owed, from bed to verse.

I will abjure the flaccid pens of fools.
My skin in parchment white; I am so fair
to want engraved inscription of a king.
Weak rhymer's wrongs he'll fiercely right and there
in princely coupling turn my figure to
a long and whelping line. 'Till then, you may
call me virgin.

FIRST LOVE

When that fat brat that toddles there is dead,
or lean or lost and all the messages we text
erased, when no one cares or knows why we
broke off, others may come to lie here on
this grass in this old park beside this lake
which we now say is our own special place.

So what? The sun is warm, the trees are green
the summer just begun. The earth is soft
beneath the sweat of flesh entwined at noon.
We'll take our time, our day, our years, why blab
of what may come? *Bug off!* Leave us alone!

SEVEN
(*Une semaine d'amour*)

I.

Green, I love your
white, sponge petal back
and your oh-so-small little
Green!
leaf wrists.

II.

Big blue birds
press in on we
and the little pink flames tickle
in their wing tips.

III.

An eager summer leaf
to fall so quickly backwards
when the sugar candy gardener
big thrusts down
the long black furrow.

IV.

Small pink spores
are to be taken
carefully with white bread
by tall tender tongues.

V.

Quick
little touches
and we fly just out the window
to paint the long warm landscape
with Chinese brushes.

VI.

In the midst of pink applesauce
sliding wetly
we drop through laughing
and do not even try to curl our toes in.

VII.

MUST
have water smooth bunches
wild yellow roses
squeezed in earth wide ribbon
to bury underneath
and breathe white water.

DON'T

No.

Don't just stand there.
Stop grinning.

Put your hand here.
No.

I mean *here*.

DOUGHNUT MAN

You just got new pink sheets,
that's why I'm here
instead of sleeping home,
doughnut man.

These sheets are smooth
as the inside of your ear,
but I'm getting crumbs
from the cinnamon frosteds

on the pillowcases and
in the still-warm wrinkles
where you were lying.
When you come back, eat the last.

You brought three–I said two–
so take the double chocolate while
I lick white sugar from pink folds,
sweet doughnut man.

I'D HATE TO SEE MY LOVE GROW OLD

I'd hate to see my love grow old,
flesh pulled by kisses, slipped, become
a simple sack of skin—dry curtained folds
so sure to part and last present the bone.

My green beginner, swing—love high, love low,
be youth-burst, love-bath breaking bud.
Love now. Love me. Love your sweet time. And so
we will hold beauty fresh at April's flood.

Yet highest loves must ebb, and staving days
when I may see your flesh hang cold,
I'll drown you young in these white marble seas,
to bed your beauty warm in brine of words.

Pale Green Good-bye

PALE GREEN GOOD-BYE

I had a quiet lover,
petal-skinned and subservient
with long fingers, trembling hands.

His body was suffused in sweats,
his way was hesitant, imploring.
He longed to be gathered in,

covered by small shells, warm tides,
green seaweed ribbons he could
flaunt as armor of compliance.

But I showered him long with
sand and laughter, sang and waved
as I ascended in a man-of-war balloon.

DRIFTING

We stood
at the edge of the surf,
the sun's rim
red behind us.

In a green wave mound
I thought I saw an arm
raised to stroke,
a seaweed strand of hair.

There was a face too,
skin white as fish belly,
and a glassy, gelatinous eye.
"What's *that*?"

I tugged your hand.
The sun had fallen,
the tide had turned.
The wind was rising.

I pointed,
you craned to see–
nothing
but sand-brown breakers.

That night
even after you
came into me,
I couldn't stop laughing.

THE STEEL PIER

The immemorial steel pier
projected far from shore
into the open ocean.

That wind-swept midnight
I hesitated while you pushed on,
calling to me to come.

Between us with a thunderclap,
part of the old pier washed away.
Nothing left but dark, rust-stained waves.

Maybe you could see what had happened,
maybe you couldn't, but you stood fast,
waved, beckoned to me to come.

I can still hear your voice,
sing-song above the breakers
calling, calling, calling.

The Crime

THE CRIME

The toxic mould of a black April
seeping through that old beachfront cafe?
Perhaps.

If I care to remember, it was I who killed him,
strangled with dry seaweed, smothered with
an anemone and a platitude.

Made afraid by the out-of-tune piano
and the smell of human beings,
I killed what I loved.

I too decked the corpse with starfish and barnacles,
closed the dead white eyes and yawned,
wondering what to do with the remains.

HAIR

Swirling about me,
I see you in the mirror
moving in long, possessive curls
down the pale curve of my back.

Caress me, beautiful brown and red.

While I sleep, you play in the sun
with secret, flowing vitality.
When I am cold, clothed in white satin,
you will run down over my shoulders.

Beautiful brown and red!

You will curl in my breast
in a hidden caress,
alive and secretly smiling
playing and moving.

Growing.

BIRTHDAY

The party's over,
guests are gone,
tables in disarray.

These lovely toys–
I like them not–
I'll rend, tear up, destroy.

I'll wait alone
for more to come
when no one's at the door,

I'll bar the windows,
break gold clocks,
nail present to before.

Still in my party dress
I stand,
violent and tall alone,

and wonder why
still no one comes
to kiss and take me home.

EPITHALAMIUM

SEA WALL

To hold the flood
I set two stones
against each other
pressing.

For years they pushed
with weights of fear
to hold back waves
of drowning.

After that time
without release
there is no sea
for diking.

Dryness remains,
the grey stones grind,
forever clenched,
contending.

SEA CALL

Break out
break forth
break through the years
let water bear away
the past, the tears,
the rigid nights,
the dark and static day.

Break out
break through
break into time–
the flow, the peause, the turn–
green waves of love
that sing and rhyme
that call, recall, return.

SOMEWHERE
A Song

Somewhere between the rocks and bricks of walls
there is a stream.
Somewhere above great monuments of stone
there lingers rain.

And when the deep wells burst
and fountains tower
brown lands will bloom with grass,
deserts will flower.

So with the earth renewed
we now may come,
like children free and sure,
returning home.

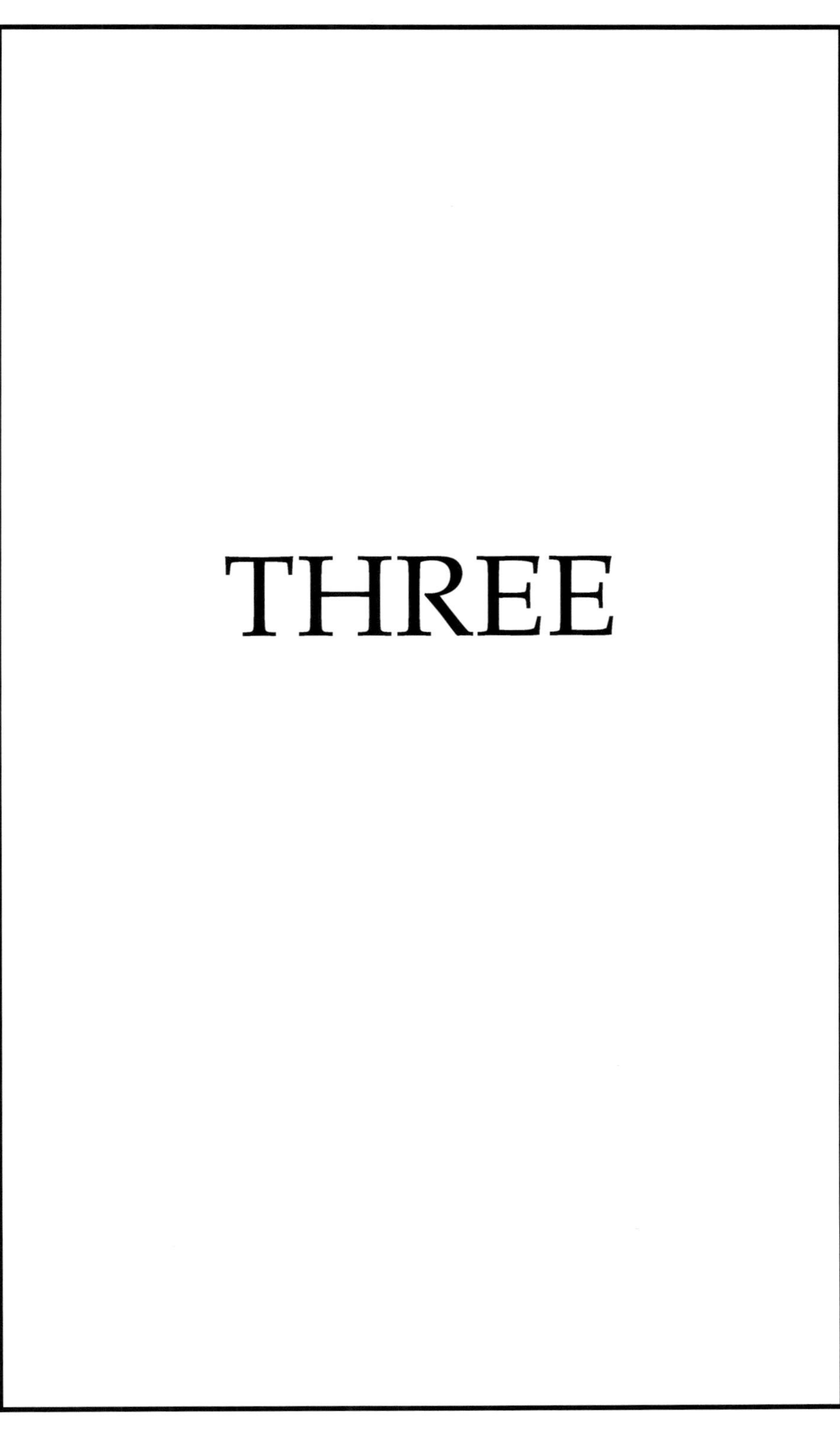

THREE

A WELCOME

Withdrawal was a looming breeze of birds
that flew-swam-rose up, shadowing the shore,
gone beyond without being counted.
They left the beach empty, without
pattern–the sure scale of spaces between wing tips.
Sand does not compose. Sand is sand.

Return is the soft-slow circle settling
down of the sea gull to the sea,
a reluctant sinking, a quiet merging,
the becoming of a vantage point, a marker.
And does the sea contain the sea gull,
or does the bird push, pattern the sea?

Can the sea encompass the sea bird,
the grey and white sea gull,
and learn to twist-turn-lunge-rise-die?
Can the sea fly? Mad melt to steam?
And when will the god grey, dirt white sea gull
rise?

IN THE DARK

In the dark between the pillows,
two heads bump, turn, kiss.
My mind drains out from
behind my eyes into your head,
trying to understand. Instead

against the invisible black ceiling
I see graceful white gulls ride and rise
on warm, teasing winds until
one dies, crumples, tumbles all the way
down to an indifferent, early morning sea.

ASHES IN A SHALLOW CUP

Ashes in a shallow cup
are silently
shifted by waves
of warm air.

The moon
is not quite full,
a bitten apple
yellow as a harvest pear.

Where are you
now that we are separated
by this sultry night
of sullen misunderstanding?

The All Day All Night

THE ALL DAY NIGHT

The night is long as night can be,
dream-wracked, intense, and warm as thought.
In pillow-tossed, blanket-lorn seas
they float, the lovers, heedlessly–
entwining, turning, melting, caught.

The dream will not release the two
but holds them spider-fast in pink
and self-spun prison. Webbed in blue
suspension, dream-bound, they now rue
the stairs behind, from which they sink.

They fall. Once more compelled, they mount
the turning stairs. They cannot stop
but seek to rise, and cease to count
time.... Dreaming, they now surmount
the final stair, attain the top.

They see the view–a yellow dream
of grey-brown seas where butterflies,
as golden leaves in summer's scheme,
will whirl and fall and falling seem
to be alive. Drawn down. Brown demise.

The morning brings a change of light
and only that. Still caught in dreams,
they wake to turn again. The flight
they crouch to mount. The day is night.
The lovers fall. Drawn down. Drowned dreams.

BITTER NOVEMBER

November recalls nothing
if not our love.
Short days, long nights,
drawn blinds, half-light.
Our confused fusion–
a blanket spread by you
against world wet, malaise
and winter cough–
November sees destroyed.

November strips us bare.
Raw, shivering, we poise
facing each other–the first time.
I feel your winter eyes,
I hide my frozen mouth
with damp, inadequate hands.
Your discontent, like brown ground,
drains each kiss cold. Bitter
November...grey branches break with snow.

WAR

I peeled your face from the squashed skull, ripped hair,
exposed the quivering privates of your brains,
a minor recompense for my heart there–
crushed in your claw, sucked out between remains
of sundered ribs, a shattered cage of blood.
We live though slain, dismembered yield
to new encounters, fall, revive on food
of hate. Can we abandon battlefields?
To die in bed–would that surfeit this love
when ravening kiss can kill, yet leave alive
its carrion? Wound in cold sheets we writhe
to rise. Transfigured worms, towards light we strive.
And from the crotch of death can life spurt forth,
flesh winter bones with grass, spring's peaceful growth?

Harpy

BETRAYAL

My sleeping love beside me lies, close-curled
and chilled in every dream. I see his face
in white retreat–lips pressed, eyes tightly furled
like petals of a frozen bud–grimace
of love encased in ice. Betrayal was
a harsh, wet wind that rode in foul and fast
from fetid seas. Puffed up with easy lies,
it rained cold piss on what we had–our past,
our halcyon years, our youth. Afraid, we froze,
now sleep entwined, trusting our stone-like form
to armor us against a break, to ice us close,
to deaden pain. Trust me, the harm is done.
I could recall–in distant time or place–
just your cold feet on mine, his insolent face.

FIRST MARRIAGE

As deadly as a soundless flood, he flows
into her fallow flesh. He fucks to kill.
He twists her limbs to his grimace, dandles
her mind between his hands and calls her "Sweet"
right to her face. He soaks within, he floods
without. Even in sleep there's no surcease.
She sinks and starts, awakes and cries to find
her body sprawled and sticky on the sheet.

Alone at noon, she tries to hide the wound,
to walk unnoticed in the world. Afraid
to flee to open sea–the drowning waves,
the purging tides–she scales harsh paths which lead
to woods, which lead to stones, which form a cairn
where water does not flow. She knows who is
the king of stones, who hides, who waits, who now
appears with outstretched, sweating, iron hands.

His touch at first is soft. It sucks her down
to lie on stones with legs apart as he
comes in–repulsive wedge that drives her down
to dreams. Yet even dreams bring no surcease.
She meets him there and yet sleeps on while he
pursues with moistened smile, presents with mock
subservience, his phallus, his pale, disgraceful
flower.

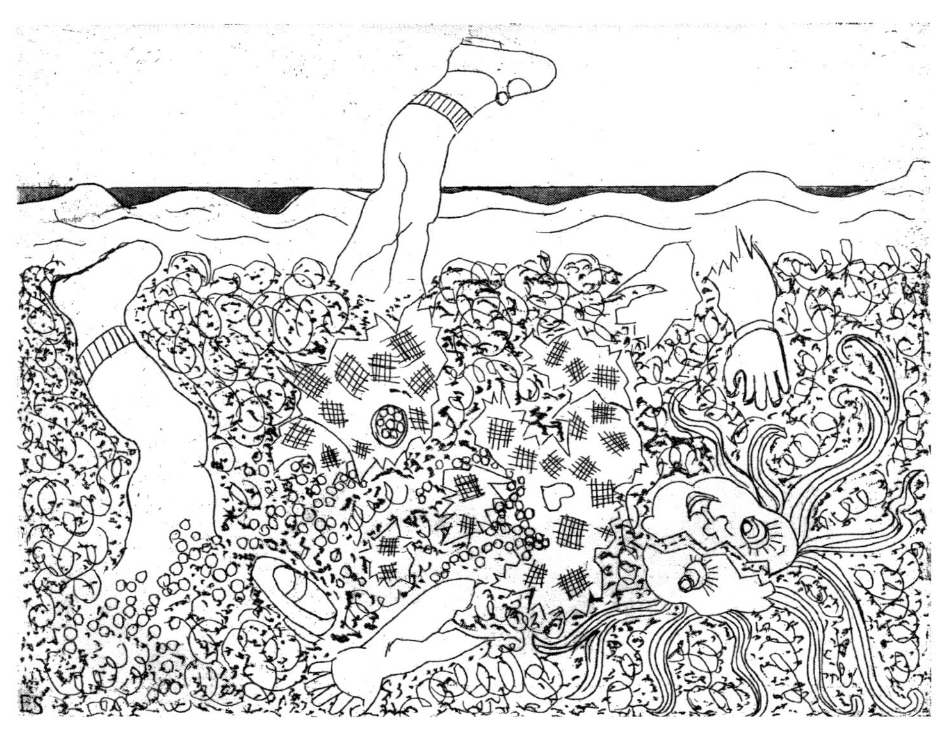

Nobody's Baby

NOBODY'S BABY

This baby doll's washed up.
Her china head is cracked,
her pretty blue eyes stuck wide.
She can't blink, she just stares up
from wet sand where waves left her.

Her sea-soaked torso's ripped,
her grey snarl stuffing scattered,
the red candy heart devoured. Yet,
from deep within her sundered form,
an old woman's voice entreats:

"Mama. Maaa-ma."

I FELL FOR YOU

I fell for you
because

you fucked (me) every night
regular

putting it in, jamming it all the way.
Even

that wasn't enough.
Stupid

as it was, I wanted you to
talk

AFTERWARDS

I like
to lie spread-eagled on rumpled sheets,
wet between the legs,
then
paste myself to your back
or
corkscrew in your arms.

You like
to get up,
pick through tumbled clothes
scattered on the floor,
find yours,
get dressed,
go home.

OUR PLACE

This was our place.
We sat in that corner
many times.

I almost expect
to see you waiting for me,
sipping coffee.

Now
I walk right by.
Sometimes I hate you

for being dead.

OLD MEN

Old men
fondle limp privates,
recall
all night encounters.

Their armpit hair
hangs loose and sparse,
dry vines
over a void.

Old men
smell old
even after they wash.
Shave lotion can't hide it.

Old man, old man,
I remember
what you were and
how you loved.

Good-bye.

FOUR

Mustache Man

MUSTACHE MAN

When we met on the boardwalk,
by chance, after all these years,
I didn't even recognize you.
You had a new, dark mustache.

Then, when I heard your voice,
things came back to me, almost forgotten
things we had told each other, lying close
on long afternoons, warm summer nights.

After we said good-bye, maybe for the last time,
(we lived far apart and were almost old)
I ran barefoot across burning sand
to wade in cooling waves.

The beach was crowded, I saw mustache men
everywhere–men of medium build and
medium weight and medium height–
men who looked a lot like you.

They were strolling, swimming, smiling or
just sitting under their beach umbrellas staring.
A dark mustache touched me softly.
That tickled. I couldn't stop laughing

until one man walked right through me,
followed by another, and another.
Then, as the tide rose and the sun sank,
they trampled me into the dark, wet sand.

OLD LOVE

You said: "Give me everything."
I almost did–what a burden!
You had a long way to go.

Afterwards, I traveled far and near.
Now, decades later, I meet you
in dreams of places I've never seen.

Sometimes, we turn away,
sometimes it's just as it was.
Nothing has changed.

SHRINE

Desire dragging will I went
in shackles to before,
to stare you down in memory
to scorn and not adore.

I passed our late contentions' bed
as if were never made,
I passed our halcyon pillow soft
where two heads once were laid.

I dreamt I slept within your arms
and slept away this time
of night long journeys to the past,
fierce rites at love's dark shrine.

The Sea Dance

THE SEA DANCE

Tonight the paper lanterns hang like slow
burned flowers tinting thick midsummer's grass
with phantom fires of early fall. They glow
upon the lean young men, who trample grass

complacently with passionate partners in
pastel–the easy young who love all night
and hold in their forever days the sun–
a seeming summer fool. They ride the white

washed waves and mold the sand, but do not see
their castles by the night ebb tide sucked down
by sinking waves. Dance drums drown out the sea;
lovers beat time and conquer all but dawn.

KEEP TIME
A Round

I am young and warm and golden
and my dress is citron chiffon,
but my silver slippers falter
as the trumpets whirl me faster,

and a stranger begs my favor,
bows and takes me from my partner,
from my lover of the summer,
to the waves' primordial murmur.

In that rhythmic, endless sea song
I hear time and death: September
soon will chill me, and the breakers'
kiss, remember, is inevitable and long.

THE CHOICE

North of the barrier island
the water chooses
to flow down
east or west of
this narrow strip of land.

But at the southern tip
where pines are tallest,
there is a reunion, a merging
as if there had never been
a division, a parting.

Like flesh, water has no memory.

Anima

ANIMA

Bury yourself in me and die,
come dream in soul's oblivion.
With me be flesh alone, while my
white sea summons you, scion, son.

I am awake, alive–crying
and biting. Rub me, scratch me. Sand
will flow, but the sea is running
under your heavy, long-fingered hand.

With me create and father all.
I call, I clasp, I sing! You drown.
Be flesh to follow me and fall,
so die with me, rise, and die again.

ENVOY: AT THE TIDELINE

I cast my works on the water–
lines, pages, books, manuscripts, fragments.
The tide retreats over warm rough sand,
flows beyond breakers to the open ocean.

Let the tide take everything. Let waves carry
dreams, forms, plots, patterns, inchoate imaginings,
words on paper, lines on copper, songs.
Good-bye to winged figures, unreal animals,

childhood scenes remembered, trees.
Good-bye characters. You can live without me.
You are strong, great shadow phantoms
who have long pursued me. *Go!*

Where to? *Away!* Go everywhere, anywhere.
Go to other countries, invade other continents.
Speak in other languages to another era. I have
done my best for you. I must rest in darkness. Let
me sleep.

Spotted Herbivorous Colophon

BOOKS BY ELISABETH STEVENS

I. Poetry:

Sirens' Songs, Baltimore, BrickHouse Books, 2011.

Sirens' Songs (*Livre d'Artiste*), Sarasota, Goss Press, 2010.

Ragbag, Sarasota, Peppertree Press, 2010.

Household Words, Sarasota, Goss Press, Second Edition, 2009.

Household Words, Baltimore, Three Conditions Press, First Edition, 2000.

The Night Lover, Delhi, Birch Brook Press, 1995.

Children of Dust: Portraits & Preludes, Baltimore, New Poets Series,. 1983.

II. Fiction:

Long Trail Winding: New & Collected Upstate Stories, Sarasota, Goss Press, 2008.

Cherry Pie & Other Stories, Baltimore, Lite Circle Books, 2001.

Eranos, (*Livre d'Artiste*) Baltimore, Goss Press, 2000.

In Foreign Parts, Delhi, Birch Brook Press, 1997.

Horse & Cart: Stories from the Country, Washington, D.C., The Wineberry Press, 1990.

Fire & Water: Six Stories, Van Nuys, Perivale Press, 1983.

III. Art and Architecture:

Ten Large Etchings by Elisabeth Stevens, Sarasota, Goss Press, 2008.

Elisabeth Stevens' Guide to Baltimore's Inner Harbor, Baltimore, Stemmer House, 1981.

Artist of Delight: A Retrospective of the Works of Keith M. Martin, 1911-1983, Baltimore, George J. Ciscle Gallery, 1987.

Prints Today: A Short Guide to the Graphic Art Market, Washington, D.C., The Washington Print Club, 1971.

Jules Bissier, 1983-1965, New York, Lefebre Gallery, 1969.

Syracuse University Press has been the distributor of seven books poetry and fiction by Elisabeth Stevens since 2007. The distributor for ***Long Trail Winding: New & Collected Upstate Stories*** *is North Country Books, and the distributor for this* ***Sirens' Songs Facsimile*** *is Istaca Books. For works unavailable from these distributors, contact gosspress@comcast.net*